WITHDRAWN

W9-CIH-250

SERIES TITLES

Cantucci, Fabiano Fabbrucci, Margherita Salvadori)
Maps: Paola Baldanzi
Photos: Corbis/Contrasto, Milan pp. 19b ©Charles & Josette Lenars, 33t ©Yann Arthus-Bertrand
Art Director: Marco Nardi
Layouts: Rebecca Milner
Project Editor: Loredana Agosta
Research: Valerie Meek, Claire Moore
Repro: Litocolor, Florence

Consultants:
MICHAEL JOHNSON is a leading expert on Native Americans. He has dedicated over 30 years of research to the subject and is the author of several books, including an award-winning encyclopedia.
Dr. JEFFREY QUITER conducts archeological research in Peru and Costa Rica but is interested in New World cultures in general. His recent interests include excavations at Moche sites and work at an early Colonial Period church in Peru.
Dr. PETER BELLWOOD is an archeologist who has been conducting research in Oceania and Southeast Asia since 1967. He is currently undertaking excavation projects in the Philippines and Vietnam. He is also interested in early farming populations all around the world.

Copyright © 2008 by McRae Books Srl, Florence (Italy)
This Zak Books edition was published 2009.
Zak Books is an imprint of McRae Books.

All rights reserved. No part of this book may be reproduced in any form without the prior written permission of the publisher and copyright owner.
All efforts have been made to obtain and provide compensation for the copyright to the photos and illustrations in this book in accordance with legal provisions. Persons who may nevertheless still have claims are requested to contact the copyright owners.

THE AMERICAS AND THE PACIFIC
was created and produced by McRae Books Srl
Via del Salviatino, 1 — 50016 — Fiesole (Florence), (Italy)
info@mcraebooks.com
www.mcraebooks.com

Publishers: Anne McRae, Marco Nardi
Series Editor: Anne McRae
Author: Sean Connolly
Main Illustrations: Alessandro Baldanzi p. 34; Giacinto Gaudenzi p. 28; Giacinto Gaudenzi and MM comunicazione 26–27; MM comunicazione (Manuela Cappon, Monica Favilli) pp. 6–7, 12–13, 36–37; Alessandro Menchi pp. 20–21; Paola Ravaglia pp. 16–17; Claudia Saraceni pp. 8–9, 22–23, 38–39, 40, 44–45; Sergio pp. 10–11, 14–15, 31, 42–43
Smaller illustrations: Studio Stalio (Alessandro

Library of Congress Cataloging-in-Publication Data

Connolly, Sean, 1956-
  The Americas and the Pacific / Sean Connolly.
    p. cm. -- (History of the world ; 6)
  Summary: "A detailed overview of the early history of American and Pacific peoples, including Native Americans, Maya, Aztecs, Inca, Aborigines, and the Maori, up to 1200 CE"--Provided by publisher.
  Includes bibliographical references and index.
  ISBN 978-8860981615 (alk. paper)
  1. Indians--History--Juvenile literature. 2. Paleo-Indians--Juvenile literature. 3. Aboriginal Australians--History--Juvenile literature. 4. Maori (New Zealand people)--History--Juvenile literature. I. Title.
  E58.4.C66 2009
  970.004'97--dc22
                                    2008008404

Printed and bound in Malaysia

HISTORY

The Americas and The Pacific

Sean Connolly

Consultants: Michael Johnson, Dr. Jeffrey Quilter, Dr. Peter Bellwood

MEMORIAL LIBRARY
500 N. DUNTON
ARLINGTON HEIGHTS, IL 60004

Zak
BOOKS

Contents

Native Americans of the Northwest Coast carved totem poles from tall trees. They were erected to serve as clan symbols, with carvings of animals such as birds and sea creatures.

Note—This book shows dates as related to the conventional beginning of our era, or the year 1, understood as the year of the birth of Jesus Christ. All events dating before this year are listed as BCE (Before Current Era). Events dating after the year 1 are defined as CE (Current Era).

TIMELINE

	60,000 years ago	40,000 years ago	8000 BCE	6000 BCE
 NATIVE AMERICANS OF THE NORTH			The Bering land bridge connects North America to the Siberian landmass.	Dogs are used as pack animals to pull sleds in the Arctic. Archaic cultures are established in the Northwest Coast.	Chumash culture develops in California.
OLMECS, ZAPOTECS, AND MAYA				
MIXTECS, TOLTECS, AND AZTECS				
 NASCA AND MOCHE CULTURE AND INCA				
ABORIGINES		People migrating from Asia become the first settlers of Australia.		
 PEOPLES OF THE PACIFIC AND THE MAORI	The first people sail from Southeast Asia to the landmass of New Guinea.	Sailors from northern New Guinea settle in the Solomon Islands.		

Introduction

The first people reached North America about 18,000 years ago, crossing the Bering land bridge which connected the continent to Asia. Over the centuries various cultures developed throughout the continent. Native Americans in the north were hunters and gatherers, and some groups, living in more hospitable lands, became farmers. Groups continued to migrate, and by 3600 BCE hunter-gatherers began cultivating crops in Meso-America (Central America). It was here that the Olmecs, Zapotecs, and Maya flourished and the Mixtecs, Toltecs, and Aztecs built their cities. In South America the Chavin, Nasca, and Moche cultures paved the way for the great Inca civilization in the Andes Mountains.

In Southeast Asia there were large migrations. Seafaring peoples reached the vast Australian continent and the western islands in the Pacific Ocean about 40,000 years ago. The Aborigines, the native people of Australia, developed into diverse cultural groups, as did the peoples of the Pacific Islands. In about 1200 CE, New Zealand was settled by the Maori, who were farmers and fierce warriors. All of these cultures were destined to change when the first European navigators reached these lands.

Aztec ceremonies included dancing and music. This drum, carved from a hollow log, depicts a person in ornamental costume, including a tassled headdress adorned with feathers.

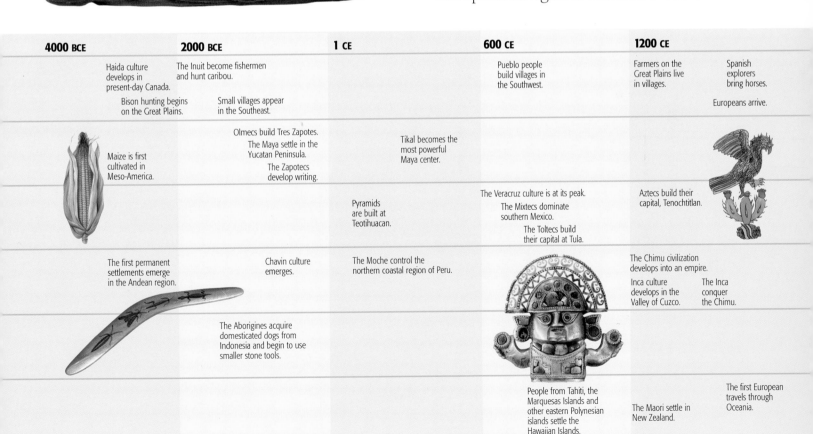

4000 BCE	2000 BCE	1 CE	600 CE	1200 CE
	Haida culture develops in present-day Canada.	The Inuit become fishermen and hunt caribou.		Pueblo people build villages in the Southwest.	Farmers on the Great Plains live in villages.	Spanish explorers bring horses.
	Bison hunting begins on the Great Plains.	Small villages appear in the Southeast.				Europeans arrive.
Maize is first cultivated in Meso-America.		Olmecs build Tres Zapotes. The Maya settle in the Yucatan Peninsula. The Zapotecs develop writing.	Tikal becomes the most powerful Maya center.		Aztecs build their capital, Tenochtitlan.
			Pyramids are built at Teotihuacan.	The Veracruz culture is at its peak. The Mixtecs dominate southern Mexico. The Toltecs build their capital at Tula.	
The first permanent settlements emerge in the Andean region.	Chavin culture emerges.	The Moche control the northern coastal region of Peru.		The Chimu civilization develops into an empire. Inca culture develops in the Valley of Cuzco. The Inca conquer the Chimu.
	The Aborigines acquire domesticated dogs from Indonesia and begin to use smaller stone tools.		People from Tahiti, the Marquesas Islands and other eastern Polynesian islands settle the Hawaiian Islands.	The Maori settle in New Zealand.	The first European travels through Oceania.

Inhabitants of the North

THE ARCTIC AND THE SUB-ARCTIC

25,000 years ago
The Bering land bridge, connects mainland North America to the Siberian landmass.

18,000 years ago
Hunters from Siberia settle in North America.

8000 BCE
Dogs are used as pack animals to pull sleds.

c. 2000 BCE
The Inuit become fishermen and hunt caribou.

c. 800 BCE
Simple pottery is made in the Arctic.

c. 450 BCE
People make special wooden utensils.

c. 1500 CE
Europeans begin to explore Canada.

Native Americans in the north inhabited the forbidding land of the Arctic and Sub-Arctic regions, adapting to cold, prolonged darkness, and lack of vegetation. Using the few materials available to them, such as animal furs and ice, they developed the kayak, harpoon, igloo, and dog-sleds more than 2,500 years ago. The hunters of the Sub-Arctic region used wood, bone, and antlers to produce tools and weapons, and canoes and toboggans to transport people and goods across a landscape of forests, plains, rivers, and lakes.

Asian hunters pursued game such as mammoths into North America, crossing Beringia (where the Bering Strait now separates the two continents). From there they followed ice-free valleys south and east into the continent.

Settling North America
For much of the past two million years, the Bering Strait has been dry. Sea levels during the Ice Age were almost 300 feet (91 m) below those of today. About 25,000 years ago, a low-lying area called Beringia, or the Bering land bridge, emerged. This land bridge allowed Asian people to migrate into North America. The Bering land bridge remained passable for 11,000 years, at the end of which rising temperatures caused sea levels to rise, covering the land bridge once more.

Many igloos included a series of domes, with separate storage areas linked to living quarters by narrow passages. A pair of experienced builders could make an entire dome in less than two hours.

A Home of Snow
The Inuit of the central Arctic region developed ice and snow houses known as igloos. These were temporary houses built during the winter seal-hunting season. Men would cut blocks of ice and arrange them in a spiral fashion until a complete dome was made. Women and children filled in cracks inside and out. Alaskan Inuit built karmaks, dome-shaped houses with frames of driftwood or whalebone, covering them with sod. These homes were partly underground, providing extra insulation from the cold.

THE ARCTIC AND THE SUB-ARCTIC REGIONS

RUSSIA

ARCTIC OCEAN

ALASKA

GREENLAND

PACIFIC OCEAN

ATLANTIC OCEAN

HUDSON BAY

CANADA

Arctic region
Sub-Arctic region

Lands of the Arctic and the Sub-arctic

The Arctic region, generally made up of flat, low-lying treeless land, is the northernmost region of the Earth. It includes modern-day northern Canada, the coast of Alaska, parts of Russia, Iceland, and Greenland. There is no real boundary between the Arctic and the Sub-arctic regions, but most agree that the northernmost tree line, of the Northern Forests, or the Sub-arctic, divides the two regions. The Sub-arctic region, which is characterized by many lakes, rivers, marshes, and forests, occupies most of modern-day Canada and Alaska.

The husky, a breed of dog that thrives in cold conditions, was the only animal domesticated by the Inuit. The dogs' keen sense of smell also helped Inuit hunters locate seals.

Inuit women spent hours making and repairing clothing. A parka— lightweight, warm, and waterproof —was the ideal outer wear for seal-hunting populations.

Dog Power

The Inuit of the Arctic region began building dog-sleds about 2,500 years ago. The best—and most lightweight—sleds had frames of driftwood, but local populations often had to use whalebones instead. Rolled and frozen seal-skin sometimes served as runners if wood and bones were in short supply. Depending on the size and weight of the sled, teams of between 6 and 16 huskies would pull it across the snow and ice.

Surviving in the North

Basic survival was a constant concern through the long Arctic winters with temperatures often averaging only -25° F (-32° C). The Inuit developed clothing that was both warm and waterproof. The basic outer garment was the parka (anorak), often made from strips of seal intestines. Seal-skins and caribou hides were also valuable materials for making trousers, mittens, and up to four layers of footwear.

This Yupik mask was made for use in dancing rituals. It represents the many spirit beings that can affect human lives.

The Spirit World

The barren lands of the Arctic and Sub-arctic regions were—to their inhabitants—full of spirits and demons. To deal with these supernatural forces, the Inuit developed a complex system of rituals and taboos. Inuit turned to shamans for advice and help in their struggle with the natural and spirit worlds. Shamans also helped people construct masks that depicted animals, spirits, or events.

THE NORTHWEST COAST AND THE PLATEAU

Northwest Coast
The Plateau

PACIFIC OCEAN

River Fraser
River Columbia
ROCKY MOUNTAINS
CASCADE RANGE
COAST MOUNTAINS

Lands of the Northwest Coast and the Plateau

The Northwest Coast is a long, narrow strip of land running down along the Pacific Ocean. It has many bays and inlets. The region has a mild, damp climate and frequent rain nourishes the abundant plant life. The Plateau is bordered by the Rocky Mountains to the east and the Cascade Range to the west. Two great rivers, the Columbia and the Fraser, run through the region which includes mountain forests, deep valleys, and large, open stretches of land.

Story-Telling

Storytellers recited tales relating to an enormously complicated mythology. Animals and fish, such as the salmon, figured heavily in these tales, which were often told during ceremonies. Listeners would be familiar with the Raven, a trickster who could either free human beings or bring about chaos. Tellers often wore masks relating to one of the characters. No two masks were the same and no storyteller ever told the whole story relating to the mask.

A wooden mask of the winter ceremonies representing the spirit of the Sun, made by the Bella Coola people of coastal British Columbia.

Potlatch guests arrive in a Haida canoe. Carved from a single cedar tree, a large canoe could hold up to 60 people. Such canoes were the mark of real wealth and power.

The Northwest Coast and the Plateau

Luxury Goods
The people of the Northwest Coast spent a lot of time making handicrafts. These goods were prized possessions and lay at the heart of a bustling trade. Many such goods were the result of long hours of manufacture. A Tlingit blanket, made from goat's wool and cedar-bark fiber, might take as long as six months to make.

A dancing shirt, woven from cedar-bark fiber and goat's wool, was one of the most prized goods a Tlingit could own. Designs depicted animal clan symbols.

Rich natural resources made hunting and fishing easy on the Northwest Coast bordering the Pacific Ocean and many peoples inhabited the region. People had time to build elaborate social systems. Craftsmen perfected the skills of working wood, while boatmen went in search of fish and even whales. But the preoccupation with wealth and social standing led to bitter rivalries and violent disputes among neighboring communities. The people of the Plateau, like those of the Northwest Coast, had plentiful sources of food, including great rivers and streams with an abundance of fish. The river systems of the Plateau facilitated trade and made cultural exchange with tribes of other regions possible.

A Display of Wealth
The woodcarvers of the Northwest Coast produced elaborately carved pieces that were either put to practical use or prized as decorative possessions. The wealthy and powerful accumulated many such goods, but they strengthened their social standing by giving them away or even destroying them. An important event such as a wedding was celebrated with a feast called *potlatch*. The host would give his prized goods to the assembled guests, ensuring his strong social position in the process.

A storage bag, made from hemp and maize husk, decorated with traditional geometric designs.

The horn of a bighorn sheep, hunted by the Plateau peoples in the mountain forests, was used to make this decorative bowl.

NORTHWEST COAST AND PLATEAU

C. 7700 BCE
Archaic cultures are established on the Northwest Coast.

C. 3500 BCE
Haida culture develops in present-day Canada.

C. 500 CE
Population increases on the Northwest Coast; elaborate ceremonies are developed.

1200–1300 CE
Permanent winter villages are established in the Plateau region.

Salmon were plentiful on the Northwest Coast, and they were important for both economic and religious reasons. People honored immortal men who had turned themselves into fish in order to feed humans.

Plateau Fishermen and Traders
Like the peoples of the Northwest Coast, the inhabitants of the Plateau were skilled fishermen. During the fishing season, from May to November, people lived beside the Columbia and Fraser rivers. They built weirs along the rivers where salmon swam upstream. Peoples of the Plateau also became great traders, taking advantage of the region's river systems to transport goods. They traded deer skins, bitterroot, hemp for making ropes, mats, and baskets.

CALIFORNIA AND THE SOUTHWEST

c. 5000 BCE
Cochise people in the Southwest cultivate vegetable crops. Chumash culture develops in California.

c. 3500 BCE
Craftsmen begin making animal figurines from twigs for ritual use.

c. 1000 BCE
Farmers in the Southwest begin to cultivate the staple crops—maize, beans, and squash.

c. 100 CE
Anasazi culture appears in the Southwest.

c. 200 CE
Cotton plant is cultivated.

c. 700 CE
Pueblo people build villages in the Southwest.

c. 1275 CE
Drought forces peoples in the Southwest to abandon villages.

c. 1600 CE
European missionaries establish themselves in Hopi areas.

CALIFORNIA AND THE SOUTHWEST

- California
- Southwest

SIERRA NEVADA MOUNTAINS

Rio Grande

PACIFIC OCEAN

Peoples of California and the Southwest

The peoples of California were hunters and gatherers. The rich and varied land of the region, running along the Pacific coast, provided a huge variety of foods. Acorns, collected from oak trees, were the staple food for many peoples. The Sierra Nevada Mountains formed the eastern border, isolating the central Californians. The arid plateaus and desert lands of the Southwest were inhabited by a surprising number of peoples who made the change from hunting and gathering to farming. The Southwest also included fertile river valleys, like that of the Rio Grande, and vast grasslands.

Baskets were decorated with geometric designs. Large ones were used for gathering and carrying seeds.

Pomo Basketmakers

A group of small tribes, called Pomo, lived near the coast of northern California. Women of the Pomo tribes made fine baskets from a number of materials such as willow shoots, sedge roots, redbud bark, and bulrushes. Baskets were used for gathering and storing food, carrying water, and even cooking.

The Kiva

The Anasazi people lived in pithouses dug into the desert and covered with thatch roofs. From about 700 CE, their descendants, the Pueblo people, began to use adobe (sun-dried mud) and stone to build above-ground living structures. Sunken chambers, called *kivas* (meaning "world below"), remained a feature of their communities. They were used as sanctuaries for spiritual rites and as a place for men to weave.

Acorns were gathered and ground into flour or meal.

Kachina dolls, representing supernatural beings, were important parts of Kiva ceremonies.

California and the Southwest

California, a land rich with natural resources, plants, and animals, was home to many peoples who, although they spoke a great variety of languages and dialects, had much in common. They were skilled basket-weavers, using a variety of materials available from the land. The desert-like landscape of the Southwest can seem as inhospitable as the Arctic, yet this region saw many developments, including the rise of agriculture. There were many different cultures, from the Navajo farmers to the nomadic Apache, who were hunters and raiders.

Below: The wooden framework was permanent while the covering was replaced each year.

Californian Homes

The native peoples of California built many different kinds of homes. The Maidu tribe in the south had one of the most unique types. They lived in dwellings that were dug into the ground and covered with mud roofs. Other tribes built dome-shaped huts with a wooden framework covered with earth, brush, bark, or reeds.

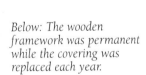

Desert Farming

Farming was not easy in the Southwest. Using complex irrigation systems, farmers were able to water the desert soil to grow maize as well as beans, squash, pumpkins, and avocados. Ceremonies were held to bring rain to the dry region and to assure a good harvest. They was plenty of work to be done throughout the year. Public ceremonies for planting, sifting, and grinding maize brought farmers together.

The Bow and Arrow

The bow and arrow was the principal weapon for hunting and warfare. Skilled hunters could pick off mountain goats, squirrels, and jackrabbits. The nomadic Apache, whose name means "enemy" in Athabascan languages, gained a reputation as fierce warriors. They used their bows and arrows to attack neighboring communities when hunting was poor or to rob them of essential supplies.

Village women of the Southwest were responsible for pottery-making, which was usually done on a roof exposed to the Sun.

Wood was scarce, so hunters needed to aim well to preserve their supply of arrows.

Stone-walled homes, called pueblos, were found in Southwest villages. These were often surrounded by farmlands, where farmers worked the dry soil with stone hoes.

The Great Plains and the Great Basin

People of the Great Plains were primarily hunters who relied on the buffalo for survival. The village was the heart of their society, acting as a center for celebrations, religious ceremonies, and trade. Women handled most of the daily chores while men went out to hunt or to gather food. The peoples of the barren desert region of the Great Basin were surrounded by little vegetation and wildlife. They foraged for edible seeds, nuts, roots, and berries. They also hunted game and caught fish.

Red stone pipe with lead inlays. Carved stems of wood were smoked as acts of friendship; these are known as "peace pipes."

Sacred Tobacco
The Great Plains people believed that tobacco had special powers–to make war or peace, to heal the sick or to ensure a successful hunt. Each man had his own long-stemmed pipe, which was his most valued and sacred possession. No fighting was allowed at quarries where men went to find stone for their pipes. The most highly prized red stone, called catlinite, came from a quarry in present-day Minnesota.

The Valuable Buffalo
The people of the Great Plains relied on the buffalo (or bison) for food, clothing, tools, and even religious ceremonies. Evidence from nearly 11,000 years ago suggests that hunters (probably disguised with buffalo hides) drove herds over cliffs or into narrow canyons. The buffalo was central to religious rites, such as the Mandan Buffalo Bull Dances, which appealed to the buffalo spirit.

The Mandan Buffalo Bull Dance combined special songs and dances in a ceremony calling for success in the buffalo hunt.

Honor Through War

All-out war between tribes was uncommon on the Great Plains, but courage and daring were highly valued. Honor came from feats of bravery called "counting coup" (from the French word for "hit"), and bravery rated higher than killing. A warrior could "count coup" if he touched an enemy during combat or if he arranged a daring escape.

Feats of bravery and daring were recorded on a warrior's coup stick, which he used to "count coup" on an enemy.

Living in the Great Basin

People living in the Great Basin had to make the best of what was available. Besides foraging for seeds, nuts, roots, and berries, tribes of the Great Basin hunted antelope, rabbits, birds and lizards. They searched for food year-round, and each season brought its own food. When men were not busy searching for food they spent time in the sweat lodge, for it was believed that sweating purified the body and spirit.

Pine nuts were gathered in September from small pine trees on the hillsides of the Great Basin.

Heat and steam were created inside the sweat lodge by pouring water over hot stones.

GREAT PLAINS AND GREAT BASIN

c. 9200–8900 BCE
Hunters and gatherers begin making stone tools.

c. 7500 BCE
The world's first cemetery is made in present-day Arkansas.

c. 3500 BCE
Bison hunting begins on the Great Plains.

c. 1500 BCE
Duck hunters in the Great Basin use duck decoys to catch their prey. Bone fish hooks are also used.

c. 700 CE
Sledges and hammerstones are used to mine salt.

c. 1250 CE
Farmers on the Great Plains live in villages.

c. 1750 CE
Spanish explorers bring horses, which are quickly adopted by the peoples of the Great Plains.

Tipi Village

The tipi was the ideal type of house for a people that was always on the move. It was easy to carry and quickly assembled. The tipi itself had spiritual meaning: its round shape echoed the sacred life circle while the floor represented the Earth where people live and the sides pointed upwards to the sky.

The opening of the tipi always faced east, away from the prevailing west winds that swept across the Great Plains.

THE GREAT PLAINS AND THE GREAT BASIN

Great Plains
Great Basin

Saskatchewan River
Lake Winnipeg
ROCKY MOUNTAINS
WASATCH MOUNTAINS
SIERRA NEVADA MOUNTAINS
MOJAVE DESERT
Rio Grande

Lands of the Great Plains and the Great Basin

The huge area of land of the Great Plains, also known as the "Great American Desert," stretches from the Rio Grande in the south to the Saskatchewan River in the north. The Rocky Mountains form the western border while a long mountain-side cliff extends to form the eastern border. The Great Plains area is a vast plateau of semi-arid grasslands. The Great Basin lies between the Sierra Nevada Mountains and the Wasatch Mountains, just north of the Mojave Desert. The region is made up of wide valleys of mostly desert land.

Peoples of the East

The eastern half of North America has borne the mark of human life for at least 12,000 years. The many peoples living among the lakes and forests of the Northeast had a profound respect for their natural surroundings. But warlike people, especially the Iroquois, would often menace their neighbors. In the warmer Southeast, Native Americans developed permanent settlements, which were larger than any others north of Mexico. These people became skilled farmers and created delicate carvings and pottery goods. In the heart of the region were the mound-builders, whose mysterious works still puzzle observers.

A carved wooden statue of a cat showing the sophistication of the early people who lived on the island of Key Marco.

Mysterious Early Culture

Key Marco lies just off the west coast of Florida. Here archeologists have uncovered traces of the early–but advanced–Calusa culture. Its inhabitants developed technology to deal with their island environment. Using tools made from shells, they built seawalls and drainage basins. Carvings, executed with sharks' teeth, show a link with cultures in the Mississippi area.

Life in the Longhouse Village

The Iroquois peoples of present-day New York State were fierce warriors who had an advanced social and political system. They lived in longhouses, built with wooden frames and covered with elm-bark. These houses, which could measure as long as 66 feet (20 m), were inhabited by large family groups. Women were at the heart of village society, owning both the longhouses and all their tools and other possessions. Men moved into their wives' longhouse when they married.

A large mortar and pestle was used to grind maize into meal.

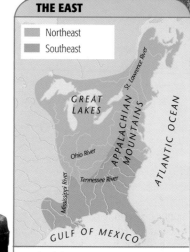

THE EAST

Northeast
Southeast

GREAT
LAKES
St. Lawrence River
APPALACHIAN
MOUNTAINS
Ohio River
ATLANTIC OCEAN
Mississippi River
Tennessee River
GULF OF MEXICO

Lands of the East

The wooded lands east of the Mississippi River were the home to many peoples. The Northeast is composed of fertile woodlands and prairies and encompasses the area of the Great Lakes, reaching to the St. Lawrence River in the north. The Southeast extends westward from the Atlantic cost to the lower Mississippi and southward to the Gulf of Mexico. The Appalachian Mountains run along the northern border of the region. Mild winters and abundant rainfall make the climate of the Southeast ideal for farming. Its forests, rivers, and streams also provided an abundant food supply.

The Cherokees, one of the largest tribes of the Southeast, built their capital city along the Tennessee River.

THE EAST

c. 2000 BCE
Copper, found in natural deposits, is used to make spearheads in the Great Lakes region.

c. 1500 BCE
Pottery appears in the Southeast.

c. 1800 BCE
Sunflowers are cultivated.

c. 1800 BCE
Axes are used to clear land and cut down trees.

c. 1500 BCE
Small villages appear in the south; circular houses are made of wooden poles and thatched coverings.

c. 700 BCE
Farmers begin to cultivate crops and build villages.

c. 200 BCE
The Hopewell people, the great mound builders, establish widespread trade contacts.

c. 900 CE
Rise of Copena civilization.

c. 1150 CE
End of Hopewell civilization.

c. 1450 BCE
Calusha peoples of the Southeast control Cushing, a site at Key Marco.

1620 BCE
European pilgrims arrive in the Mayflower.

The basic equipment for the game of lacrosse has changed little since the sport was developed by the native peoples of Canada.

Lacrosse

The Algonquian peoples of Canada developed a stick-and-ball game called baggataway to train young men to become warriors. Villages competed against each other in warlike matches. French-Canadians later called the game "lacrosse" because the netted stick resembles a bishop's cross.

Effigy Mounds

For thousands of years, the people of the Ohio and Mississippi valleys built huge earthwork mounds along ridges and high ground. The purpose and shape of these mounds differed—some had buried artifacts, others were used as burial sites. Later examples, known as effigy mounds, were built in the shape of people, birds, panthers, and snakes.

The meaning of Ohio's Great Serpent Mound— built by the Adena people and stretching nearly 1,760 feet (400 m) —remains a mystery.

Green Maize Rite

The Creek, Shawnees, Cherokees, and other Southeastern farmers prized maize as a crop. In late summer, as the last of the maize was ripening, they held the Green Maize Rite. Spread over several days during the full Moon, this ceremony gave thanks for the harvest and ushered in a new year. The rituals and dancing ended with a feast featuring maize prepared in many forms.

The most sacred part of the Green Maize Rite was the dance around a ceremonial fire. Coals from the fire were used to light village hearths, signalling the beginning of a new year.

Ancient Meso-America

Evidence suggests that the first human inhabitants of Meso-America were descendants of Asian peoples who crossed the Bering land bridge (see page 5). Fanning out southward and eastward, they arrived in present-day Mexico many thousands of years ago. These first settlers were hunters and gatherers, but eventually they developed settled communities based on cultivation of crops such as maize. The Olmecs and the Zapotecs were two of the first cultures to develop in this region.

MESO-AMERICA

3600 BCE
Maize is first cultivated in Meso-America, signaling the permanent change from hunter-gather culture to farming.

2300 BCE
The first permanent farming communities develop in southern Mexico. Pottery is first developed at about the same time.

1400 BCE
The Olmecs begin to cultivate maize.

1200 BCE
The first Olmec ceremonial center is built at Tres Zapotes near the coast of the Gulf of Mexico.

1000 BCE
The Maya people begin to settle in the Yucatan Peninsula of southern Mexico.

c. 800 BCE
The Zapotecs develop Meso-America's first writing.

500 BCE
The Zapotecs build the mountain-city of Monte Albán as political states develop in the Oaxaca Valley of southern Mexico.

MESO-AMERICA

GULF OF MEXICO

CHICHEN ITZA

YUCATAN PENINSULA

TRES ZAPOTES

LA VENTA

SAN LORENZO

OAXACA VALLEY

MONTE ALBÁN

SANTA CRUZ

PACIFIC OCEAN

Area of Olmec influence
Area of Maya influence c. 1000 BCE
Area of Maya influence c. 800 BCE
Area of Zapotec influence
● Sites settled by, or influenced by the Olmecs

Meso-American Cultures

Few settlements developed in the towering mountain ranges that run the length of Meso-America, but civilizations took root in some of the more welcoming landscapes in the region. The Olmec and Zapotec cultures developed in the south, near the coast of the Gulf of Mexico. Jutting northeast from that area is the Yucatan Peninsula, the tropical home of the Maya civilization (see map on page 19). The fertile Valley of Mexico, high on a plateau, was the cradle of other Meso-American civilizations—including the Aztecs (see page 29).

The Olmecs

Olmec culture developed in about 1100 BCE in southern Mexico, an area of prime maize-growing country which provided the Olmecs with an ample supply of food and, ultimately, time to devote to other pursuits. The Olmecs created some enduring works of art, many of them featuring remarkable depictions of humans and animals. Some were modelled from clay; others were carved from stone and precious minerals. Huge, brooding stone statues of human heads were probably created to commemorate noted Olmec chieftains and hereditary leaders.

A giant Olmec head, found at La Venta. It was carved from a single piece of basalt that was dragged to the site.

Early Writing

The Zapotecs were the first in Meso-America to develop a writing system. (It would be expanded by the later Maya civilization). By about 800 BCE, the Zapotecs were using a system of hieroglyphs. Recognizable images and patterns of images clearly spelled out important details of Zapotec warfare, business, religion, and culture.

Stone slab with Zapotec carving and writing depicting a bride and groom at their wedding (top) and a female and male ancestor (lower level). Running around these images is a border of hieroglyphs that include the names of 13 relatives of the newlyweds.

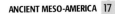

The Wonders of Maize

The transition from hunting and gathering to farming came between 7000 and 2000 BCE as the Meso-American climate became drier. Settlements became more stable as flood plains dried out enough to become cultivated. People began cultivating avocados, squash, pumpkins, beans, and maize. By about 1500 BCE, about 40 percent of the Meso-American diet was made up of maize. Ample rainfall and constant heat allowed up to four crops of this nutritious grain each year.

Maize became (and remains) the staple grain of farming communities in Central America. It can be eaten fresh or dried and ground into flour for baking.

The Zapotecs at Monte Albán

Some of the most extensive Meso-American buildings are found at the site known as Monte Albán, the Spanish name for a mountain-city in the southern highlands of Mexico. Monte Albán was the center of the Zapotec culture, which flourished in the Oaxaca Valley from 500 BCE to about 750 CE. More than 30,000 people lived in this administrative and cultural center. About 2,000 stone-carved houses surrounded a vast main plaza. Huge staircases led from the plaza to temples and a ceremonial ball-playing court. Throughout the city, warriors and deities were commemorated in stone wall carvings.

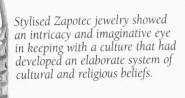

Stylised Zapotec jewelry showed an intricacy and imaginative eye in keeping with a culture that had developed an elaborate system of cultural and religious beliefs.

The massive city of Monte Albán stood on the top of a flattened mountain. The scale of the city and its central plaza is huge. The plaza alone measures 984 x 492 feet (300 x 150 m).

Maya Society

The most sophisticated of the Pre-Columbian civilizations of Meso-America was developed by the Maya. They had settled the humid tropical lowlands of the Yucatan Peninsula by about 1000 BCE. Within a few centuries they began draining swamp land, making it into arable farming land. Initially absorbing the advances of the neighboring Zapotecs, they went on to develop a network of prosperous communities. Maya civilization became noted for its works of art and architecture. Extensive trading networks linked communities throughout their region, although these same communities often engaged in bitter warfare.

The Maya had no metal tools. Artists carved stone using stone tools. The figure depicted in this jade mask is wearing typical Maya ceremonial headgear, including heavy earplugs.

Maya Artists

The Maya developed a distinctive artistic style using many different materials, including wood and stone sculpture, murals and pottery. Most of the wooden sculpture has decayed, but limestone carvings and bas-reliefs are full of ornamentation and intricate carving. Murals depicted religious and historical themes while colorful examples of pottery have been found as ornaments in many Maya graves.

Trade

Although the Yucatan Peninsula does not have a rich supply of natural resources, the Maya still managed to develop lucrative trading links based on their local goods. Salt was one of the few natural resources that the Maya traded. Along with chocolate, colorful feathers, and slaves, the Maya traded salt for essential items such as copper tools. The dense tropical forest made passage difficult, so much of this trade was carried out by boat—either by river or along the coast.

This chocolate container dates from around 500 CE. The Maya ground cacao beans into a paste, which they then mixed with hot water to make drinking chocolate.

This Maya mural depicts a group of merchants, guarded by their patron god "The Black Scorpion" (the dark figure in the center). He was also the guardian of cacao, a prized trading good.

Expert Farmers

The lands of the Yucatan Peninsula are not ideal for farming, but the Maya adapted to them successfully with a number of intensive farming techniques. Swamps were drained to open up farmland while areas of thick jungle were cut down with stone axes. The felled trees were burned, depositing soil-enriching ash on the cleared land. Maya farmers also created terraces on sloping terrain to gain more growing space.

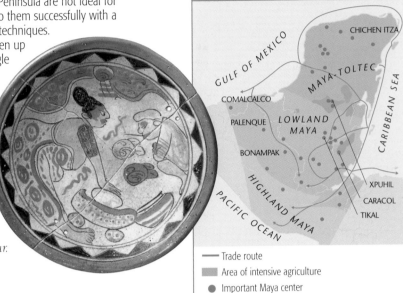

This elaborately decorated Maya pottery bowl shows a woman grinding maize into flour.

THE LAND OF THE MAYA

CHICHEN ITZA

GULF OF MEXICO

MAYA-TOLTEC

COMALCALCO

PALENQUE

LOWLAND MAYA

BONAMPAK

CARIBBEAN SEA

XPUHIL

CARACOL

TIKAL

HIGHLAND MAYA

PACIFIC OCEAN

— Trade route

▪ Area of intensive agriculture

● Important Maya center c. 290–790 CE

Maya Civilization

The area covered by the Maya civilization extended across the Yucatan Peninsula in present-day southern Mexico and Belize, and as far as Guatemala, Honduras, and parts of El Salvador. Most of the region is low-lying, except for the gentle highlands of the region where Mexico meets Guatemala. A number of tribes speaking similar languages settled there. The Maya, the largest tribe, has given its name to both the language group and the civilization of the region.

Warfare

Maya civilization was not centralized under one acknowledged leader. Instead, independent city-states shared a culture and trading links and often went to war with each other. The purpose of these conflicts was not to gain territory so much as to capture soldiers. Captives either became slaves (who could be traded) or were sacrificed to the gods.

In 1946, archeologists discovered a vivid mural covering several walls of a ceremonial building at Bonampak, in southern Mexico. The colorful images depict battle scenes during a Maya dynastic struggle of 792 CE.

The Maya Way of Life

The Maya lived in a number of separate, and independent, city-states, which were ruled by kings. Some of these counted as many as 90,000 inhabitants. Nobles lived in elaborate and highly decorated houses, while ordinary people dwelled in simple, single-room homes made of wood and adobe. Daily life revolved around tending crops and domestic animals. Women were concerned with raising the family, while men hunted and engaged in sports, especially the mysterious ball game played on large L-shaped fields.

Family Life

Maya children underwent a baptismal rite conducted by a priest and village elders. Maya notions of beauty called for the flattening of the front and back of the head, done at an early age when a child's skull was still soft. Older people filed their teeth and often had tattoos. Crops included cotton, cacao beans, papaya, and avocado. The resin of copal trees was used as chewing gum. Hunters would venture into the forest with atlatls or blow guns to kill deer, wild boar, and birds.

This musical whistle, dating from around 700 CE, is carved in the shape of a Maya couple. The Maya devoted much energy to planning and celebrating weddings.

Many familiar fruits and vegetables are native to the Meso-American region and would have been cultivated by the Maya. They include (clockwise from top) yellow and green peppers (capsicums), avocados, cactus leaves, and tomatoes.

This small statue shows a Maya woman weaving on a hand loom almost identical to those still in use in parts of southern Mexico today.

Maya Homes

Many of the stone-built palaces of Maya nobles still stand, but ordinary people lived in houses that were built of organic materials that soon rotted in the tropical climate. However, some modern houses in rural Yucatan still have features that probably date back to ancient Maya times. Thatched houses, in a rounded rectangular shape, were built on low platforms surrounded by a small walls that marked the edge of each family's property.

Apart from the house itself, an ordinary Maya property would include a small garden, well, chicken coop, and latrine.

Maya Women

Strict cultural traditions dictated the roles of men and women in Maya society. The household took the father's name, which was passed down to his sons. Women were in charge of the household and raising children. While boys were allowed greater freedom and the chance to live together learning fighting and hunting skills, girls remained at home under supervision. There they would learn cooking, weaving, and other household skills. Many of these customs remain common in modern Yucatan.

Sacred Sport

The Maya and other Meso-American people played a sport on large courts bounded by tall walls. Two teams would compete to drive a hard rubber ball through a stone hoop high up on a wall. The sport had religious significance because the Maya believed it tied in with the natural cycles of the seasons and the heavens. The captain of the losing team was sometimes sacrificed after the match.

This stone carving from Bonampak, southern Mexico, depicts a royal ruler in ceremonial attire with jewelry made of precious stones.

Injuries were common in the Maya ball game, so players usually wore heavy belts and other protective clothing.

Maya Royalty

Over the centuries, the Maya developed a number of beliefs concerning royalty. The most important was the belief that people of royal blood were direct descendants of the gods. In life and in death they were considered different from ordinary people. Members of the royal family were expected to offer their blood in religious ceremonies. The royal dead were buried in temple pyramids while ordinary people were laid to rest under the floors of their homes.

A series of intricately carved Maya hieroglyphs.

The Maya Alphabet

The Maya developed a written alphabet that was based on hieroglyph principles. By about 100 CE, the system was in common use throughout the region. Overall, about 1,000 different signs were used to represent gods, animals, and other features of the observable world. This writing system remained a mystery until archeologists realised that the signs were of two types—either pictorial representations of the things themselves or symbols for spoken words.

Recorded Knowledge

Much of what the Maya wrote—often on bark, which rots away over time—has been lost. However, four codices have survived along with the many detailed stone carvings on walls and monuments. A fuller picture of Maya life is emerging as it becomes apparent that scribes recorded not just history, astronomy, and prophecies, but many details of how political life operated in Maya society.

A decorative bowl showing a Maya scribe at work. Apart from the scribes themselves, only priests and noblemen could understand the Maya script.

A codex was written on thin strips of fig tree bark and folded into an accordion shape to create pages. The glyphs were read from top to bottom and left to right.

Maya Achievements

The Maya created one of the most advanced civilizations in Meso-America—and in the ancient world. They used some existing knowledge, such as the Zapotec hieroglyphic writing system, as a springboard for their far more intensive investigation and recording of the world around them. Many of their most notable advances came in the fields of technology, astronomy, arithmetic, and architecture. They developed a complex calendar which was linked to heavenly motion. Maya temples represented the peak of their scientific and technological skills. These buildings show remarkable adaptability in using available building materials, often in remote locations.

Counting Innovation

The Maya were brilliant mathematicians, and as in so many other developments, arithmetic was linked to other fields of knowledge such as astronomy and the calendar. Numbers were recorded in a pattern of dots, dashes, and a stylized shell. Maya mathematicians understood the concept of zero, allowing them to represent (and understand) huge numbers with relatively few symbols.

Maya symbols representing the numbers. A dot represented the number one and a bar stood for five.

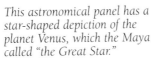

This astronomical panel has a star-shaped depiction of the planet Venus, which the Maya called "the Great Star."

Watching the Stars

The passage of the Moon, planets, and stars was important to the Maya, who combined astronomical observation with astrological beliefs. Their advanced calendar allowed them to predict eclipses and other heavenly occurrences with great accuracy. Priests almost certainly doubled as astronomers, making their observations from the tops of temples high above the surrounding trees.

The Maya Calendar

The Maya were able to record time with amazing accuracy, using their mathematical and astronomical skills to produce a calendar as sophisticated as most in use today. They represented their calendar on two types of wheel, each indicating 20-day months. One wheel had 13 months; the other had 18 (with eight "unlucky" days added to make a solar year of 365 days). Each day within a 20-day cycle had special significance, carrying with it traditions of good or bad luck.

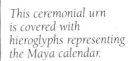

This ceremonial urn is covered with hieroglyphs representing the Maya calendar.

Building Technology

Maya architects used local building materials to produce impressive results. Limestone was cut into blocks, which fit together neatly. The builders laid some of these blocks in a staircase-like pattern—each side jutting out to meet over a passage—to create corbelled vaults. Lime-based plaster coated walls, staircases, and even the base of plazas to create a smooth finish. Many temples and palaces were decorated with reliefs.

The graceful temples of Palenque, in the modern Mexican state of Chiapas. Inside the Temple of Inscriptions (shown here in a cutaway view) archeologists found the sarcophagus of a Maya king, K'inich Janaab' Pakal I (reigned 615–683 CE).

Maya Beliefs and Rituals

The Maya Pantheon

Archeologists are still puzzled by the vast number of Maya deities. Some of the confusion arises because many of the deities were considered to be up to four different individuals, and sometimes a deity had a male and a female aspect.

A ceremonial incense burner depicts Itzamna as an old man with a crooked nose. The Maya believed that Itzamna named all the Maya villages and cities.

MAYA DEITIES

Itzamna
The most important deity and creator of the Universe. He is credited with inventing writing and is the patron of science and learning.

Ix Chel
Rainbow deity and wife of Itzamna. The Maya believed that Ix Chel and Itzamna were the parents of all the other deities. She is also the deity of weaving, medicine, and childbirth.

Chac
The benevolent rain deity, whose intervention was often sought by Maya farmers.

Yum Kaax
Deity of maize and patron of husbandry.

Yum Cimil
A death deity. He had many forms, one of which presided over the nine underworlds.

Buluc Chabtan
A war deity, associated with violent death and human sacrifice.

R eligion played an important—and often terrifying—part in the everyday life of the Maya. The blood of royal people and outright human sacrifices were regular features of religious ceremonies that were dictated by the seemingly infallible Maya calendar. The arrival of solar and lunar eclipses, as predicted by the priests' calendar, served to reinforce belief among the people at large. A vast number of gods and goddesses represented the forces that had the greatest impact on the lives of the people. Most of these were gods of rain, sunshine, and other natural forces. Others included an array of deities associated with the animals native to the tropical Yucatan environment.

The Role of Priests

Maya priests all came from the noble class, and their sons usually succeeded them in office after a long period of training. Priests were charged with linking the complicated network of religious rites and ceremonies with the intricate Maya calendar. In this regard, they were also responsible for recording and predicting the astronomical events that intrigued the Maya. Like other shamans, Maya priests regularly used substances to achieve an altered state of being.

By using substances which changed their state of being, Maya priests believed that they could get in touch with the supernatural forces. The Maya used alcoholic beverages made from maize, honey, tree bark, and other plant materials. They interpreted their experiences to predict future events.

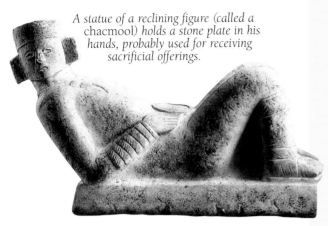

A statue of a reclining figure (called a chacmool) holds a stone plate in his hands, probably used for receiving sacrificial offerings.

Human Sacrifices

The Maya deities demanded regular sacrifices to ensure peace and prosperity. Archaeologists believe that the earliest Maya societies sacrificed only plants and animals, but over time the practice of human sacrifice became widespread. The usual victims were captives or slaves, but sometimes illegitimate children were sacrificed in religious ceremonies. The sacrifice of royal blood was believed to be especially effective. Priests would hold down the victim's arms and legs while another would open up the chest above the heart.

Below: A vase depicting a Maya priest conducting a religious ceremony. The priest is wearing parts of a slaughtered jaguar as leggings (including the tail) and mittens.

Royal Blood

Since royal people, according to Maya belief, were descended from one or more of the gods, royal blood was considered especially important in religious ceremonies. Blood-letting rites, taking blood from a city-state's own ruler, were carried out on special occasions. Blood was spattered on thin bark or passed down hollow tubes into special vessels. Captured nobles and royals were also sacrificed, with their hearts placed in special statuary bowls.

A carved relief shows a ruler holding a torch while his wife passes a thorn-studded rope through her tongue to extract blood.

Royal Maya women clad in white garments perform the blood-letting ritual in this detail from a wall painting at Bonampak, Mexico. They are gathered round a throne and are attended by a male servant holding a sharp object.

Animal Powers

Animals played a large part in everyday Maya life, both for their practical contribution and for their religious significance. Effigies of dogs have been found in Maya burial sites, signaling their importance in the journey to the afterlife. Other animals had more mystical significance. The armadillo, for example, was associated with the Maya underworld. The jaguar, also associated with the underworld, was admired for its stealth, cunning, and deadly power.

A stylized statue of a jaguar, the jungle creature that the Maya admired and feared the most.

The Largest City in America

Teotihuacan developed in the first century CE, with massive temples forming its core. The Pyramid of the Sun— the third-largest pyramid in the world —stood 200 feet (60 m) high and was aligned with the rising and setting Sun on the summer solstice. Teotihuacan flourished for five centuries as an important regional center and one of the largest cities in the world. From 650 CE it was attacked repeatedly, and by about 750 CE, Teotihuacan was largely destroyed and abandoned.

Mexican Empires

Elsewhere in Meso-America other cultures achieved a high degree of development. They borrowed ideas from each other and from the people they conquered. To the north of the Maya region lay the city-state of Teotihuacan, built around a vast city that supported a population of perhaps 200,000. Veracruz culture developed along the Gulf of Mexico and in southern Mexico the Mixtecs took over the site of Monte Albán. The Toltecs, warriors from northern Mexico, migrated south to the Valley of Mexico.

Teotihuacan attracted craftsmen from a wide region. This unusual chicken-shaped ceramic container is decorated with jade and colorful shells.

A broad thoroughfare called the Avenue of the Dead ran between the ceremonial buildings of Teotihuacan. Temples dedicated to different deities were built on the flat tops of the pyramids.

MESO-AMERICAN CULTURES

EL TEUL

TAMUIN

TOLLANTZINCO

TULA

EL TAJIN

CHAPULTEPEC

CULHUACAN

TEHUACAN

TEOTITLAN

MONTE ALBÁN

SAN LORENZO

PACIFIC OCEAN

- Teotihuacan
- Spread of Teotihuacan culture
- Veracruz
- Spread of Veracruz culture
- Monte Albán
- Spread of Monte Albán culture
- Toltec area
- Toltec capital

Mexican Empires

Meso-America can be divided into two main areas: the Maya and the Mexican. Cultures in each group had similar languages, religious beliefs, writing systems, and artistic styles. Although independent city-states were the hallmark of the Maya (eastern) region, large empires developed in the Mexican (western) region, where Teotihuacan and the Toltec capital of Tula developed in the Valley of Mexico. Monte Albán (center of Zapotec and Mixtec culture) was in the southern highlands, near the Pacific coast. The Veracruz culture flourished on the Gulf coast, east of the Valley of Mexico.

Chichen Itza

Chichen Itza, built around sacred wells in the northern Yucatan Peninsula, began as a Maya center around 500 CE. Pilgrims came to make offerings to the rain deity. By the late 600s it was abandoned by the Maya, but around 300 years later it was rebuilt by the Itza tribe (after whom it is named). Toltec invaders from neighboring Tula conquered it around 1200 CE, adding to it over the next two centuries.

Chichen Itza means "mouth of the wells of the Itza." Pilgrims from all over the region came to the Sacred Well of Sacrifice to make offerings, like this intricate carving, to the deity of rain.

Veracruz Culture

El Tajin was the centre of the Veracruz culture. Within the city, several courts were designed for the ceremonial ball game developed by the Maya (see page 21) and popular throughout Meso-America. Carvings represent the protective equipment worn by the players. Pottery from the Veracruz lowlands shows a distinctive style called Remojadas, in which objects are depicted realistically but embellished with geometric designs.

This stone carving represents a protective yoke worn by players around the waist in the ceremonial ball game at El Tajin and elsewhere in Meso-America.

A hummingbird perches on the rim of this highly decorated Mixtec cup. The distinctive Mixtec "step fret" geometric motif is visible just above the base.

The Mixtecs of Monte Albán

The Mixtecs of southern Mexico became known as the best craftsmen in the region. They used diplomacy and arranged marriages with conquered rivals to secure a homeland, with the former Zapotec city of Monte Albán as one of its centres. The Mixtecs recorded their military and political history in colourful pictographs. They were also noted for their metalwork, stonework, mosaics, pottery, embroidery and weaving.

Toltec craftsmen celebrated their culture's warlike reputation. This ornament represents a coyote warrior, whose face peers out from the open jaws of a coyote mask.

Warriors of Tula

The warlike Toltecs migrated south to the Valley of Mexico after the decline of Teotihuacan in the 8th century CE. They built a new capital, Tula, and controlled the first military empire in the region. The Toltec civilization declined in the 12th century as other peoples invaded and sacked Tula. Some of the Toltecs moved further south and were absorbed by the Maya.

THE AZTECS

c. 1150 CE
Nomadic hunters known as the Aztecs (or Mexica) move south into the Valley of Mexico. The leaders of several existing city-states employ them as mercenaries.

c. 1325
Aztec priests spot an eagle devouring a snake on a rock by Lake Texcoco, fulfiling a prophecy that they would build a civilization there. Work begins on draining land and building the capital, Tenochtitlan, on islands in the lake.

c. 1350 CE
Using Tenochtitlan as a base, the Aztecs begin to conquer most of their neighbors in the Valley of Mexico, extracting tribute as they build an empire based on military might.

c. 1500
The Aztecs overcome the two other powers—the Texcoco and Tlaleloco—with whom they had shared control of the empire. The Aztec-ruled territory extended from today's central Mexico to the Guatemalan border.

A farmer poles his flat-bottomed boat along a canal running between cultivated areas. The chinampas, which had begun as rafts, were eventually anchored to the shallow lake bottom.

A carved calendar stone reflects the circular passage of time in the Aztec calendar.

Stone Carving

Stoneworking was important to the Aztecs. Their huge capital city, Tenochtitlan, was built from stone that was quarried and cut into massive blocks. Stone carvings served religious and historical purposes. The complex Aztec creation myth stated that the Earth had undergone a series of destructions and reconstructions. These were plotted and recorded on stone carvings representing the Aztec calendar.

Aztec Origins

Waves of newcomers flooded into the fertile Valley of Mexico after the fall of the Toltec civilisation in the 12th century CE. The nomadic Aztecs—among the last to arrive—were forced to establish themselves on the swampy western shore of Lake Texcoco. However, the Aztecs would turn this hardship into a real advantage, reclaiming land for farming and for their capital, Tenochtitlan. With this easily defended city as their base, the warlike Aztecs proceeded to conquer their neighbours and to establish a powerful empire that still held sway when the Spaniards arrived in the early 1500s.

A legend told that the Aztecs would build a great civilization when they saw a cactus growing out of a rock and an eagle perched upon it. Aztec priests claimed to have seen this vision on the shores of Lake Texcoco.

Agricultural Innovations

Despite their justified reputation as fierce warriors, the Aztecs were also excellent farmers. They reclaimed low-lying marshland by the shore of the lake for farming. Networks of canals drained excess water, gaining more arable land. Seeds of corn and other crops were sown in raised fields called *chinampas* (meaning "rafts"), which ran between rows of trees. The rich soil between the rows of trees came from sediment and mud extracted from a neighboring canal.

Aztec warriors wore uniforms that indicated their military rank. Those who had captured many enemy warriors were entitled to use highly adorned shields like this one, made of jaguar skin and feathers.

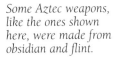

Some Aztec weapons, like the ones shown here, were made from obsidian and flint.

Aztec Warriors

The Aztecs prized bravery and military success among their warriors. Aztec wars were fought for many reasons—to gain military control, new farming land, or to find captives to be used as slaves or sacrificial victims. Exceptional bravery allowed soldiers to join one of two highest military orders, the otomies or the "shorn ones." Members of these orders had special privileges, which included being able to drink *pulque*, a beer-like beverage, in public.

Aztec Religion

The Aztecs had a complex religion that absorbed many beliefs of the peoples they conquered. Aztec myths number at least 1,600 different deities, and these deities could assume many forms. One of the most important gods was Huitzlipochtli, the god of war and the Sun, who guided the Aztecs on their journey to the Valley of Mexico. His name comes from the Aztec word for "hummingbird," reflecting the Aztec belief that warriors were reborn as hummingbirds.

This Aztec mask of Tezcatlipoca, the deity of destruction, was made by laying precious stones over a human skull.

AZTECS IN THE VALLEY OF MEXICO

TENOCHTITLAN
CHICHEN ITZA
TEXCOCO
YUCATAN PENINSULA
ITZA
NACO
MIXCO VIEJO
IXIMCHE
PACIFIC OCEAN

■ Aztec empire under Itzcoatl 1427–1440 CE
■ Aztec empire under Moteuczoma Ilhuicamina 1440–1468 CE
■ Aztec empire under Axayacatl 1469–1481 CE
■ Aztec empire under Ahuitzotl 1486–1502 CE
■ Aztec empire under Moteuczoma Xocoyotl 1502–1520 CE
● Aztec province
■ Independent Maya states
● Major Maya center

Aztec Origins

Aztec civilization developed at a troubled time in Meso-American history. Other peoples had taken over the cities and farming lands of the declining Toltec and Maya civilizations. The Aztecs, who numbered only a few hundred at first, settled on inferior land and initially acted as mercenaries for the Tepanec, a neighboring people. As they gained in power and confidence, they turned on the Tepanecs and went on to conquer other Mexican peoples as they built up an empire of their own.

Aztec Society

Tenochtitlan was a thriving metropolis that supported a population of locally born people as well as slaves and traders from the more remote areas under Aztec control. Although the Aztecs had no knowledge of the wheel, the 300,000 people living in the city found a constant supply of new goods at the markets. These markets drew thousands of people, including many who had walked long distances from outlying cities. Running through the heart of Aztec society at the same time, though, was a profound awareness of religion, with its ceremonies, rituals, and taboos.

A page from the Codex Mendoza, a 16th-century Spanish manuscript recording Aztec customs, shows girls being taught cooking and weaving skills.

Class System

Aztec society was divided into three well-defined classes. People of a certain class could be identified by their clothing, housing, and even the foods they ate. At the top were the nobles and members of the royal family. Only they could wear elaborate feathered outfits. Below them —making up the majority of the population— were commoners. Within this group there were further subdivisions based on profession or military success. At the bottom were serfs who worked for others.

The headdress of Emperor Moctezuma II (reigned 1502–1520 CE) was 4 feet (1.2 m) high and made of bright green quetzal feathers. Gold disks and blue plumes added a further note of status.

Children and Family

Family life was important to the Aztecs, and several families would live together in a single household. The arrival of a new child was a joyous occasion. The Aztec baptismal ceremony welcomed the child into society, laying out tools appropriate to the sex of the child—weapons for a boy, weaving and cooking tools for a girl. Older children were given household chores such as carrying loads or helping to prepare food. Punishments for misbehavior included spanking, pinching, or even being held over a fire of roasting chili peppers.

A stone carving of an Aztec mother holding two children. Mothers were highly respected, and immediately after childbirth they would be applauded as warriors who had "captured" a child.

Aztec Ceremonies

Religion was an essential part of everyday Aztec life. Sacrificial ceremonies were conducted to placate the gods. Death and blood-letting played an important part in the Aztec belief that the gods had shed their blood in creating the world. Offerings of blood were a way of repaying the gods for their sacrifice. The Aztecs also performed elaborate sacrifices to the deity Huitzlipochtli (see page 29) to ensure that the Sun would return each morning. Fertility deities, as well, played an important part in Aztec rituals since terrible droughts often threatened Aztec life.

Victims to the gods were stretched out across a special stone and their hearts were torn out with a sacrificial stone knife like this one.

Aztec Markets

Trade was a vital component in the success of the Aztec empire. Crops, precious jewels and feathers, artwork, and even slaves, were transported great distances to Tenochtitlan and other Aztec centers. Canoes laden with market goods crowded the canals running through the island capital. People came to buy and sell, but also to exchange information about events occurring far from the heart of the Aztec domain.

The distinctive orange and black Aztec pottery has been found throughout Mexico, giving evidence of the extensive Aztec trading links.

As many as 60,000 people crowded into some markets on a main market day.

Chavin stone carving of the Staff God, showing the intricate detail that is a feature of all Chavin artwork.

Chavin Culture

Chavin culture was widespread across the Andean region, reaching its peak about 900–200 BCE. Its highly developed artwork indicates a religion based on the worship of animals such as eagles, jaguars, and snakes. Like the Olmec culture in Meso-America (see page 16), Chavin culture initiated many of the beliefs and cultural traditions that later Andean civilizations preserved and developed. Temples and stone carvings discovered across northern Peru give an idea of the extent of Chavin influence.

This whale ivory statue shows the Nasca practice of tying boards to an infant's skull to produce a slanted forehead.

This Paracas-style garment, from the southern coast of Peru, was found in a tomb. It shows a highly developed artistic sense coupled with exquisite workmanship.

Peoples of the Andes

Like other peoples of the Americas, the settlers in the South American Andes were descendants of Asian hunters and gatherers who had crossed the Bering land bridge (see page 5). By about 3500 BCE, some of these settlers had begun to establish permanent farming settlements. These early farmers defied the harsh, high-altitude conditions to cultivate native plants such as potatoes, beans, peppers, and maize. Many settlements grew into cities, some numbering thousands of inhabitants, in the high Andean valleys and along the coast. The ruins of these cities offer some information about these ancient cultures, but much still remains to be learned. Pottery and other artifacts—many found at burial sites—have shed some light on these mysterious early cultures.

Nasca Culture

The Nasca culture flourished along the southern coast of Peru from about 200 BCE to 600 CE. Faced with a forbidding land, the Nasca people built aqueducts to irrigate their desert farmland. Their large settlements—some probably with populations of 8,000 or more—have been described as South America's first cities. They created monumental architecture as well as highly decorated pottery. The Nasca also left behind huge geoglyphs. Some of these are zigzags, spirals, and other geometric patterns; others take shape of animals.

THE ANDES

c. 3500 BCE
The first permanent settlements, based on farming begin to emerge in the Andean region.

c. 900 BCE
The Chavin culture, which influenced most later Andean civilizations, begins to emerge and lasts for about 700 years.

c. 200 BCE
The Nasca civilization begins to flourish along the southern coast of Peru.

c. 100 CE
The Moche people begin to control the northern coastal region of Peru after the decline of the Chavin culture.

c. 850 CE
Work begins on Chan Chan, which becomes the capital of the Chimu civilization.

c. 1200 CE
The Chimu civilization develops into an empire.

1470 CE
The Chimu empire is conquered by the Inca.

Many of the mysterious Nasca lines, drawn across the desert floor, can only be deciphered from above.

Gold and turquoise figures, such as the one shown here, formed the handles of Chimu ceremonial knives.

Moche Warriors

The Moche civilization emerged as a power around 100 CE, after the decline of the Chavin culture in the same region of Peru. Like the Nasca to the south, the Moche people constructed large irrigation systems. They were also fierce warriors. Painting, pottery, and ceramic sculpture show Moche myths as well as their devotion to fighting. Some of the most dramatic images show prisoners of war being sacrificed.

This ceramic Moche sculpture vividly depicts a prisoner of war bound to a stake and waiting sacrifice.

Chimu Gold

The Chimu developed the dominant Andean culture around 900 CE, reaching a peak in the 14th and 15th centuries. The Chimu kingdom extended across much of coastal Peru. The Chimu developed extensive irrigation works to create a flourishing agricultural economy in the semi-arid landscape. The ruins of the Chimu capital, Chan Chan, are among the largest archeological sites in South America. The Chimu were eventually defeated by the Inca (see page 34) around 1470 CE.

This ornate pair of sculpted golden arms shows the artistry and metalworking skills of Chimu craftsmen.

THE INCA EMPIRE

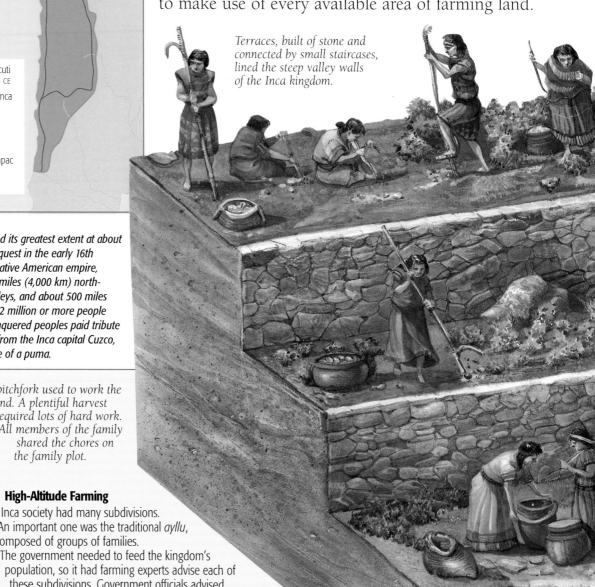

QUITO

CUENCA

SOUTH AMERICA

CHAN CHAN • CAJAMARCA

HUANUCO
BOMBON

MACHU PICCHU

PACHACA MAC •
INCAHUASI

OLLANTAYTAMBO
CUZCO

VILCASHUAMAN

LIMATAMBO

TIAHUANACO

PACIFIC OCEAN

Inca Empire under Pachacuti
Inca Yupanqui 1438–1463 CE

Growth under Pachacuti Inca
Yupanqui and Topa Inca
1463–1471 CE

Growth under Topa Inca
1471–1493 CE

Growth under Huayna Capac
1493–1525 CE

Imperial roads

The Inca Empire
The Inca Empire had reached its greatest extent at about the time of the Spanish conquest in the early 16th century. It was the largest Native American empire, extending more than 2,500 miles (4,000 km) north-south along the Andean valleys, and about 500 miles (800 km) east-west. Some 12 million or more people lived within the empire. Conquered peoples paid tribute to the Inca and were ruled from the Inca capital Cuzco, which was built in the shape of a puma.

The Rise of the Inca

By about 1200 CE, a new group of people had emerged as the dominant power in the Andes. These people spoke a language called *Quechua*. The term "Inca" is used to refer to both these people and their emperor. From their capital of Cuzco, high in the Andean valleys, the Inca extended their influence along much of western South America. They were skilled farmers, producing enough food to support a large population. Inca farmers cultivated the dizzyingly steep mountain slopes, building terraces to make use of every available area of farming land.

Terraces, built of stone and connected by small staircases, lined the steep valley walls of the Inca kingdom.

A pitchfork used to work the land. A plentiful harvest required lots of hard work. All members of the family shared the chores on the family plot.

High-Altitude Farming
Inca society had many subdivisions. An important one was the traditional *ayllu*, composed of groups of families. The government needed to feed the kingdom's population, so it had farming experts advise each of these subdivisions. Government officials advised farmers on which crops to grow, how to irrigate and fertilise their land, and how to construct stone terraces. In return, the government took a share of the harvest, which was then doled out where it was needed.

Mountain Animals

Alpacas, llamas, vicunas, and guanacos—all members of the camel family—were domesticated by the Andean people as early as 4500 BCE. These sure-footed mountain animals were ideal for carrying loads along steep and narrow mountain paths. They also provided a source of food and their wool was used to make clothing. Few other animals were domesticated, although the Inca and other Andean peoples ate guinea pigs as a source of protein.

The Inca held their growing empire together by strong military force. A strong standing army quickly quashed rebellions. Soldiers were armed with wooden-handled clubs and axes (above left). They could also tie stone stars (above right) to a cord and swing them at enemies.

The Inca rarely used alpacas— which are smaller than llamas —as beasts of burden. Instead, alpacas were herded and shorn for their soft, silky wool.

THE INCA

c. 1200 CE
Inca culture develops in the Valley of Cuzco.

1438 CE
Pachacuti Inca Yupanqui takes the throne.

1471 CE
Pachacuti Inca Yupanqui dies and his son, Topa Inca, becomes emperor after the defeat of the Chimu.

1525–1527 CE
When the last of the great emperors, Huayna Capac, dies of smallpox in 1525, civil war over succession breaks out.

1532 CE
Atahualpa takes the throne after the civil war but is soon killed by an attack by the Spanish conquistador, Francisco Pizarro (c. 1471–1541).

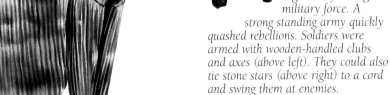

This Moche vessel shows people making chicha, a drink made of pounded maize or cassava tubers mixed with water or even saliva.

The potato, a staple crop which can withstand harsh climates, made life in the highlands possible for the earliest settlers.

Inca Food

The Inca exploited all available farming land; they even carved terraces along the steep valley walls of their kingdom to extend the area under cultivation. An extensive irrigation system brought water to drier areas, sometimes passing along the terraces. Inca farmers cultivated potatoes, squash, pumpkins, beans, and many other native plants. Maize was an essential grain and could also be used to make a beer-like drink called *chicha*, which was often used in religious ceremonies.

Inca Stonemasons

Like their predecessors, Inca stonemasons used hammers made of stone that was harder than the pieces being carved. Large blocks of stone were carved into shape and then dragged to the site where they would be used. Architects used small-scale models to give builders an idea of the intended outcome. Blocks of stone were laid out, fitting together neatly without mortar. Inca buildings had no windows. Doors had a trapezoid shape—rough rectangles with the tops narrower than the bottoms.

The Gateway of the Sun at Tiahuanacu, in modern-day Bolivia, was built in the 9th century by a pre-Inca culture. Carved from a single piece of stone, it stands 12 feet (3.7 m) high and weighs 9 tons.

Featherwork

The cultures of Meso-America and the Andes all valued the highly colored plumage of tropical birds. The Inca, like some other cultures, developed techniques to weave feathers together to create clothing, headdresses, or ceremonial clothing to be worn on special occasions. They also worked feathers together, gluing them onto hard objects to create mosaics. Feathers from coastal birds, such as parrots and macaws, were highly prized and were transported long distances into the mountains for use in the Inca capital.

This Inca poncho has stylized images of owls and fish woven into its design. Each of the feathers was chosen for its size and color before being woven into the cloth.

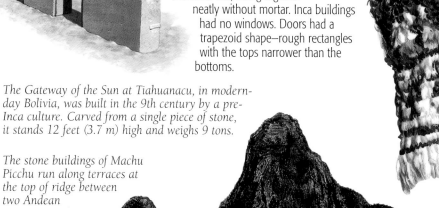

The stone buildings of Machu Picchu run along terraces at the top of ridge between two Andean mountains. The River Urubamba flows 2,000 feet (600 m) below the city.

Cities in the Sky

The Inca city of Machu Picchu lies high on a mountain ridge about 50 miles (80 km) northwest of Cuzco. Machu Picchu was discovered by the an American explorer in 1911, having remained hidden since the arrival of the Spanish nearly 400 years before. The origins and purpose of Machu Picchu —which is remote even by Inca standards—remain a mystery. Archeologists believe that the "sky city" may have had a mainly religious or spiritual function.

Ingenuity in the Andes

The near-vertical mountain slopes, the lack of rain, and the bitter winter temperatures all make the Andes an unlikely location in which to build an empire. But the Inca managed to overcome these obstacles with a remarkable number of ingenious inventions and building techniques. Despite their lack of sophisticated tools or a written language, Inca officials oversaw massive building and road projects that linked the furthest outposts of the empire to the capital at Cuzco. Roads were built along the Andean slopes and rope bridges spanned the valleys that could not be connected by roads. Craftsmen and artisans created clothing and works of art that stand comparison with any created elsewhere in the world. Ingenious methods of transportation and communication enabled the Inca to trade within and govern their far-flung empire.

Road Systems

The Inca Empire was connected by a road network spanning 15,000 miles (25,000 km). Stone-built roads were constructed by teams of people serving out their government labor. These roads helped to defend the empire and to ensure the flow of goods that kept the economy going. Government officials carrying information about harvests, tributes, and reports on building progress also relied on this safe communication system. The Inca had no horses or wheeled vehicles. However, teams of trained runners, working in relays, could carry information up to 250 miles (400 km) a day.

Travel by Water

Although the Inca capital was located well inland from the ocean, the Inca established a complex trading system along the Pacific coast. Using boats made from reed, they conducted business up and down the coast with large fleets of these trading vessels. One of the most highly prized traded goods was the spiny oyster, native to the waters off Ecuador. Its red shell was considered sacred and even believed to bring rain.

Larger Inca trading boats were reinforced with balsa-wood logs and had cabins to house the crew and to store the goods being shipped.

Plan of Cuzco, the Inca capital, showing the main roads which led out of the city.

The Inca kingdom pioneered the use of the first suspension bridges, which played a vital role in connecting the extensive road network.

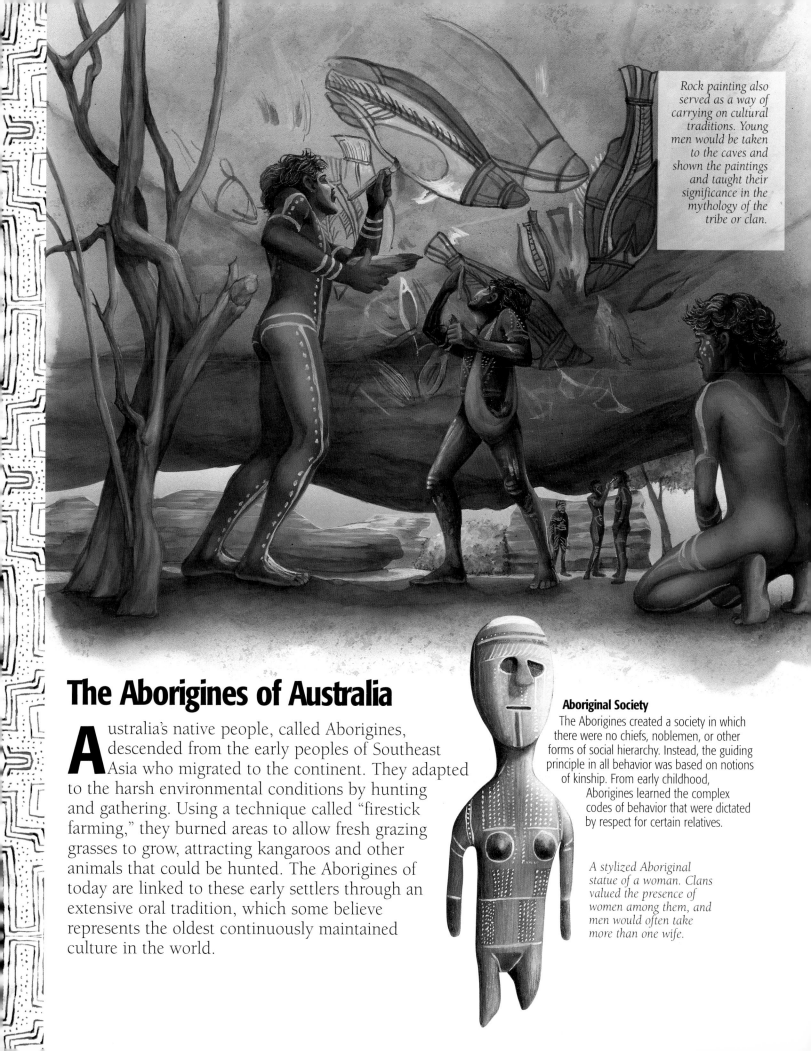

Rock painting also served as a way of carrying on cultural traditions. Young men would be taken to the caves and shown the paintings and taught their significance in the mythology of the tribe or clan.

The Aborigines of Australia

Australia's native people, called Aborigines, descended from the early peoples of Southeast Asia who migrated to the continent. They adapted to the harsh environmental conditions by hunting and gathering. Using a technique called "firestick farming," they burned areas to allow fresh grazing grasses to grow, attracting kangaroos and other animals that could be hunted. The Aborigines of today are linked to these early settlers through an extensive oral tradition, which some believe represents the oldest continuously maintained culture in the world.

Aboriginal Society

The Aborigines created a society in which there were no chiefs, noblemen, or other forms of social hierarchy. Instead, the guiding principle in all behavior was based on notions of kinship. From early childhood, Aborigines learned the complex codes of behavior that were dictated by respect for certain relatives.

A stylized Aboriginal statue of a woman. Clans valued the presence of women among them, and men would often take more than one wife.

Rock Painters

The Aborigines used natural pigments to create painted images on rock walls, usually in caves or rocky overhangs where they took shelter. The walls were sometimes decorated with engravings. These images were tied to the Dreamtime myths and combined realistic portrayals of hunters and prey with more abstract, geometric designs. The less realistic aspects of these rock paintings is believed to be linked to magical qualities inherent in the spirit creatures, qualities that can bestow luck on hunting or other human activities.

Bark painting was one of the most common forms of Aboriginal artistic expression. Like other art forms, such as music and dance, painting had a spiritual dimension. This painting stresses the spirit of the hunted emus rather than their physical appearance.

The nomadic Aborigines enjoyed the chance to trade goods, such as this mother-of-pearl pendant, with other groups when they met on social occasions.

Aboriginal Festivals

When food was plentiful, groups of hundreds of Aborigines would join together for social gatherings called *corroborees*. Singing and dancing were the main features of these gatherings, with men from different groups or clans showing off their dancing skills to the beat of clapping, singing, or the music of the didgeridoo.

The didgeridoo, made from a hollow log, was widely played in gatherings in northern Australia. It was also associated with ceremonial music.

Boomerangs designed to return to the thrower were lighter than the hunting versions. Aborigines used them for amusement or to frighten birds into nets laid as traps.

Hunting and Weapons

Hunting and gathering were the source of food for Aborigines. Men were skilled at tracking prey such as kangaroos, wallabies, and emus over long distances. They would kill the animal by throwing clubs, woomeras, or boomerangs. Aborigines also built fish traps in rivers and lakes. Women did most of the food gathering, using stone axes to reach small mammals, birds' eggs and bees' nests in hollow trees. People also gathered nuts, berries, and other fruit.

THE ABORIGINES

c. 40,000 years ago
People migrating from Asia become the first settlers of Australia.

c. 30,000 years ago
Most parts of Australia are settled by the Aborigines.

c. 25,000 years ago
Harsh climatic conditions cause Aborigines to abandon the arid interior of Australia, reoccupying it 10,000 years later when conditions improved.

c. 13,500–8,000 years ago
Rising sea levels cause Tasmania to become an island, isolating the Aboriginal population from the mainland.

c. 2000 BCE
The Aborigines introduce the dingo, or domesticated dog, to Australia. At the same time, they begin to use small, flaked stone tools.

1788 CE
At the time of the first European settlement, Aboriginal culture had diversified, with more than 200 languages spoken.

The Dreamtime

Aboriginal religious belief centers on the idea of Dreamtime, a complex view of the world that combines the past, present, and future. They believe that mythic creatures created the Earth and all life, leaving behind a set of rules on how to preserve this legacy. Aboriginal religion and art carries on the traditions and ceremonial duties associated with Dreamtime.

This bark painting depicts a Wandjina, an ancestral being associated with the Dreamtime and believed to control rainfall and the fertility of animals.

MIGRATIONS TO AUSTRALIA

INDONESIA

NEW GUINEA

PACIFIC OCEAN

AUSTRALIA

INDIAN OCEAN

TASMANIA

— Maximum extent of Sunda Landmass c. 20,000 BCE

— Maximum extent of Sahul Landmass c. 20,000 BCE

→ Probable migration routes

● Human presence before 20,000 BCE

● Human presence after 20,000 BCE

Populating the Continent

Asian settlers were the first human inhabitants of Australia, arriving around 40,000 years ago, although some evidence suggests that they arrived long before —perhaps as early as 60,000 years ago. Lower sea levels at that time shortened the sea crossing distance between the Sunda landmass (Asia) and the Sahul landmass (Australia and New Guinea).

THE PACIFIC

c. 40,000–60,000 years ago
The first people sail from Southeast Asia to Australia and New Guinea.

c. 28,000 years ago
Sailors from northern New Guinea voyage east and settle in the Solomon Islands.

c. 3,500 years ago
Settlers from Southeast Asia settle the group of islands in the Bismarck Sea and then move eastward to settle Fiji, Tonga, and Samoa in central Polynesia.

c. 600 BCE
The Society Islands, the group containing Tahiti, in eastern Polynesia, are settled.

c. 600–1250 CE
Polynesians from Tahiti, Marquesas, and other eastern islands sail more than 2,000 miles (3,200 km) to settle the Hawaiian Islands.

1521 CE
Portuguese explorer Ferdinand Magellan (c. 1480–1521), on his round-the-world voyage, becomes the first European to travel through Oceania.

Pigs were an important commodity and were only killed on special occasions. They were slaughtered with special hammers like this one from Vanuatu (in Melanesia), carved with two ancestral faces— one facing down at the pig and the other facing up at the holder.

THE PACIFIC

The Divisions of Oceania
The Pacific, largest of the Earth's oceans, covers more than a third of the surface of the planet. Oceania is subdivided into three main areas. Melanesia includes the large island of New Guinea and other islands in the western Pacific south of the Equator. Micronesia lies in the northwest of Oceania as far north as the Tropic of Cancer. Polynesia covers the vast southern and southeastern area of Oceania. It makes up a huge triangle, with New Zealand, Hawaii, and Easter Island considered to be the three points. Most of Oceania has a tropical climate, with regular heavy rain, although the northeast is drier but prone to sporadic fierce storms.

Migration routes with dates

Polynesia

Micronesia

Melanesia

Ancestor Worship

Despite being dispersed across a vast region, the inhabitants of Polynesia had a number of cultural similarities. Chief among these was ancestor worship. This formed the core of religious beliefs and practices on the islands. People believed that the spirits of the dead were spiritual beings that could still play a part in everyday life. They would keep reminders of dead relatives to consult on important matters.

The Pacific Islands

Volcanic activity produced—and continues to shape—many of the islands of the Pacific Ocean. There are more than 30,000 islands, most of them small or of moderate size. Together, these islands are known as Oceania. Some islands, such as Tahiti and the Hawaiian Islands, are actually the tips of huge mountains that rise up from the sea floor. Others, called atolls, are ring-shaped coral reefs which once surrounded a mountain that has sunk back into the sea. The far western islands (near New Guinea) of this vast collection of scattered islands were the first to be settled between 40,000 and 60,000 years ago.

The people of New Guinea believed that a dead person's skull provided a link between that person's spirit and the present. Skulls were ritually washed and adorned with feathers and colorful shells.

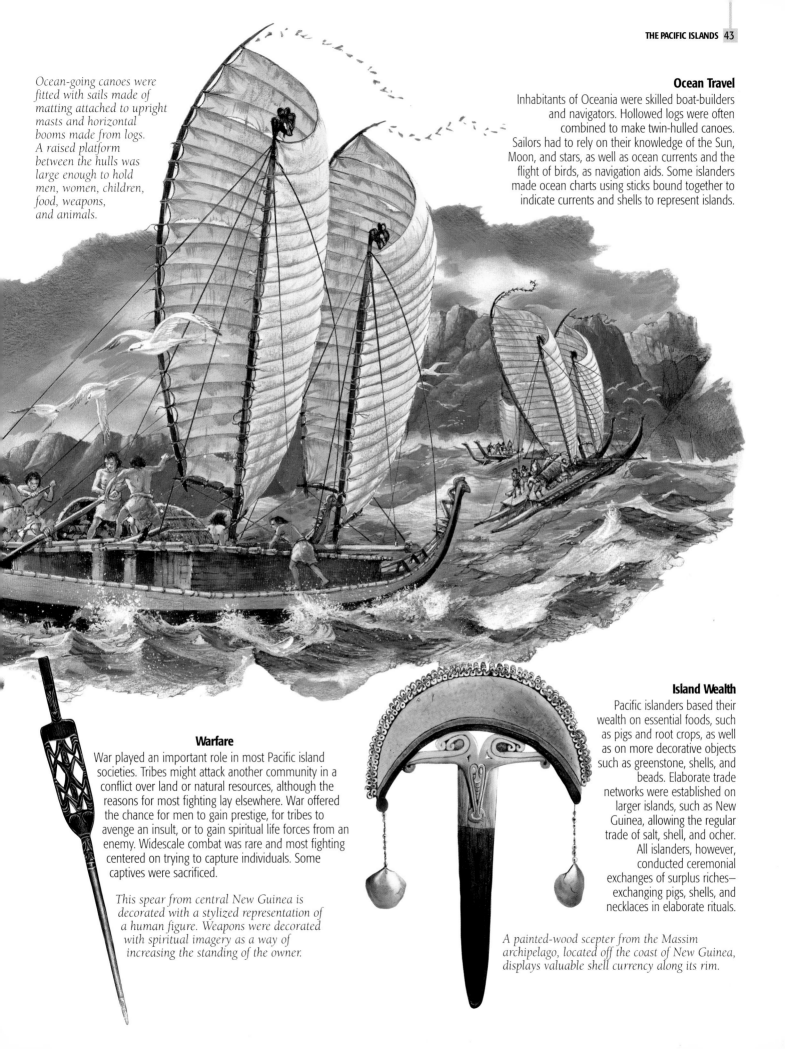

Ocean-going canoes were fitted with sails made of matting attached to upright masts and horizontal booms made from logs. A raised platform between the hulls was large enough to hold men, women, children, food, weapons, and animals.

Ocean Travel

Inhabitants of Oceania were skilled boat-builders and navigators. Hollowed logs were often combined to make twin-hulled canoes. Sailors had to rely on their knowledge of the Sun, Moon, and stars, as well as ocean currents and the flight of birds, as navigation aids. Some islanders made ocean charts using sticks bound together to indicate currents and shells to represent islands.

Warfare

War played an important role in most Pacific island societies. Tribes might attack another community in a conflict over land or natural resources, although the reasons for most fighting lay elsewhere. War offered the chance for men to gain prestige, for tribes to avenge an insult, or to gain spiritual life forces from an enemy. Widescale combat was rare and most fighting centered on trying to capture individuals. Some captives were sacrificed.

This spear from central New Guinea is decorated with a stylized representation of a human figure. Weapons were decorated with spiritual imagery as a way of increasing the standing of the owner.

Island Wealth

Pacific islanders based their wealth on essential foods, such as pigs and root crops, as well as on more decorative objects such as greenstone, shells, and beads. Elaborate trade networks were established on larger islands, such as New Guinea, allowing the regular trade of salt, shell, and ocher. All islanders, however, conducted ceremonial exchanges of surplus riches— exchanging pigs, shells, and necklaces in elaborate rituals.

A painted-wood scepter from the Massim archipelago, located off the coast of New Guinea, displays valuable shell currency along its rim.

The Maori built large baskets to trap fish along the coast and in rivers.

The Maori of New Zealand

The native inhabitants of New Zealand —the Maori—arrived around 800 years ago. The Maori brought with them the domesticated Polynesian dog along with important food plants such as the kumara (sweet potato), taro, and yam. As well as cultivating these staple crops, the Maori adapted to their new surroundings by hunting and fishing. Their culture was warlike, with an emphasis on pride and honor. Insults, often arising from long-standing feuds, were avenged violently. All men were warriors, who prepared for battle with the ceremonial *haka* dance. As a result, the Maori fortified their towns against attack.

The Maori Arrive in New Zealand

Archeology indicates that New Zealand was settled by the Maori in about 1200 CE. They arrived from central Polynesia, perhaps the Cook or Society Islands. Several canoes might have been involved in the early voyages.

The wooden stern piece of a Maori canoe. The Maori valued their canoes highly and decorated them with traditional circular motifs.

Maori Villages

With warfare so common, the Maori tribes would build a stockaded defensive area called a *pa*, where villagers could congregate during fighting. Ditches and banks added to the defensive strength of a *pa*. Residential houses were built in the more open village, called a *kainga*. Houses in the *kainga* all surrounded a public plaza. Villages also had a *pataka*, or storehouse for preserved foods and weapons. Carvings on the *pataka* honored village ancestors and celebrated the status of the chief.

The village pataka stood on raised piles, several feet off the ground, and was located in the central plaza, or marae. The pataka had special significance for the Maori, who rated it second only to war canoes in terms of social status.

EARLY SETTLEMENT OF NEW ZEALAND

- Main areas of settlement c. 1300 CE
- Main areas of agriculture and fortification c. 1700 CE
- Southern limit of sweet potato crop cultivation

NORTH ISLAND

SOUTH ISLAND

TASMAN SEA

PACIFIC OCEAN

Early Settlers

The first Maori were voyagers from the Polynesian islands of the Pacific Ocean; the Polynesians themselves were descendants of people who had originated in Southeast Asia.

THE MAORI

c. 1200 CE
The first permanent settlers, Polynesian navigators from the Pacific region, arrive in New Zealand and establish the Maori culture. They arrive in large, ocean-going canoes and establish coastal settlements, especially along the temperate east coast.

c. 1500 CE
The Maori construct over 5,000 earthwork pa in the North Island and northern South Island. Many of these still survive today.

c. 1350 CE
Maori tradition cites this time as the date of the "great fleet" of canoes bringing large numbers of new immigrants from Polynesia.

Late 18th and early 19th centuries
European whalers and missionaries establish the first white settlements in New Zealand. They are opposed—often fiercely— by neighboring Maori.

The Maori hunted moas, New Zealand's flightless birds, to extinction.

Maori Hunters

When the early peoples settled in New Zealand, large, flightless birds similar to ostriches, called moas, inhabited the land. Some of the largest moas were up to 6.6 feet (2 m) high. The moas were hunted by the Maori settlers who were probably armed with spears and hunting dogs. Moas provided not only a good source of food, but their bones were used to make weapons, tools, and jewelry.

Facial Decoration

Men of high social standing often had tattoos on their thighs and faces. The circular designs of head tattoos, unique to New Zealand, had symbolic significance. Tattoo artists were highly respected, and were considered *tapu*, or sacred. They used bone chisels to dig patterns in the skin and then rubbed in soot to make the designs permanent.

A carved wooden head displays the distinctive circular facial decorations of the Maori.

Artwork

Wood carving was subject to *tapu*, the spiritual rules placing restrictions on aspects of Maori life. Felling trees was considered to be cutting down a descendant of the god of forests and humanity; even woodchips falling from carving could not be burned or discarded. The lizard was the principal feature in Maori carving. Craftsmen also shaped greenstone from the South Island for use as tools, war clubs, and pendants.

Distinctive Maori hei tiki pendants were carved from greenstone. The human-like figure was considered to have great power.

Glossary

Aqueduct A system of channels, pipes, bridges, and canals, which carries a water supply to a town or city.

Arable Suitable for farming.

Archeologist A scientist who studies the remains of ancient peoples, such as tools, weapons, pots, and buildings, to learn more about cultures of the distant past.

Archaic Term used to describe something from an early period. Something very old.

Archipelago A group of small islands in an area of sea.

Astronomy The scientific study of the Sun, Moon, stars, and other heavenly bodies.

Basin An area of land which is drained by a river and its streams.

Clan A group of people belonging to the same tribe who are related or share a common ancestor.

Climate Weather conditions, including temperature, rainfall (or snowfall), and wind of a particular region over time.

Codex (plural codices) A handwritten book or set of manuscripts from ancient times.

Commodity A valuable item usually traded for other goods or sold for profit.

Crop A plant or its product, such as grain, fruit, or vegetables, grown by farmers.

Decoy A living or fake animal used by hunters to attract or lure prey into a trap.

Delta A triangle-shaped area of land near a river where the waters flow into the sea or ocean.

Diplomacy The art and practice of forming and maintaining good relations with other countries or people.

Domesticate To tame and bring animals and plants under control so that they can live with and work for people.

Eclipse An eclipse occurs when a heavenly body, such as the Sun or Moon, is positioned between a source of light and another heavenly body. A lunar eclipse, for example, occurs when the Moon lies between the Earth and the Sun, blocking sunlight on Earth for a brief moment.

Effigy A representation of a person or spirit used for ritual purpose.

Epic A long poem which tells the story of gods and heroes or the history of a nation or people.

Extinct Term used to describe species of animals or plants that are no longer living.

Forage To search for and collect food.

Geoglyphs Drawings done on the Earth.

Geometric Term used to describe something decorated with or having the form of simple shapes such as squares, triangles, and circles.

Gulf Part of a large body of water that is surrounded by land on three sides.

Habitat The environment or natural surroundings where plants or animals live.

Hieroglyph A symbol used to represent a word or idea.

Ice Age A period of Earth's history in which huge sheets of ice cover a vast part of the Earth's surface.

Irrigation The process of bringing water to fields.

Mercenary A paid professional soldier who fights for a foreign country.

Mine A deep hole or a network of underground tunnels made for the extraction of minerals or metals.

Missionary One who is sent on a mission to a foreign land to educate or convert people to a particular religion.

Mummification The process of preserving a dead body to prevent it from decaying.

Nomadic Term used to describe people who move from place to place in search of pastures for their animals. People who wander and do not settle down in any particular place.

Pictograph A picture representing a word or idea.

Pigment Any colored substance used to make paint or a colored mixture. A natural substance which gives color to plants and animals.

Pioneer To begin or participate in the development of something new. One who discovers new ideas, fields of study, or technology. One of the first settlers in a new or unknown land who prepares the way for others.

Plain A vast or large, flat, area of land, usually without trees.

Plateau An elevated, relatively flat, stretch of land.

Prairie An area of flat, grassy land with few trees.

Pre-Columbian Word used to describe culture, peoples, or society in the Americas before the arrival of Christopher Columbus (1451–1506), an Italian explorer who sailed to the Americas in 1492. Cultures of the Americas before European contact.

Pyramid A large, four-sided triangular stone building constructed in ancient times. In ancient American cultures royal people were buried in pyramids.

Sanctuary A sacred, holy place or temple.

Scribe In ancient times, a person who wrote down or recorded important events. A person who copied important documents or manuscripts.

Shaman A priest who is believed to be able to contact the spirit world and who practices magic to heal, predict the future, and control natural events.

Sledge A hammer with a long handle and heavy head used to pound stakes or wedges into a surface.

Staple The principal crop grown in a region which is the basic food supply, such as rice or corn.

Succession The process in which a person inherits a title after the death of a king or ruler. The order in which this occurs.

Index